A Slice THROUGH A City

PETER KENT

Published in the United States in 1996 by

The Millbrook Press, Inc.
2 Old New Milford Road
Brookfield, Connecticut 06804

First published in Great Britain in 1995 by

Macdonald Young Books
Campus 400
Maylands Avenue
Hemel Hempstead HP2 7EZ

Commissioning Editor: Thomas Keegan
Editor: Jill A. Laidlaw
Designer: Simon Borrough
Illustrator: Peter Kent

Library of Congress Cataloging-in-Publication Data
Kent, Peter.
    A slice through a city/Peter Kent.
        p. cm.
    Originally published: Hemel Hempstead: Macdonald Young
    Books, 1995.
    Includes bibliographical references and index.
    Summary: Detailed cross-sections show a city from the
Stone Age to the twentieth century, including the structures
which are raised and torn down, the people who inhabit the
city, and an accumulating underground collection of artifacts.
    ISBN 0-7613-0039-2 (lib. bdg.)
    1. Cities and towns–History–Juvenile literature.
2. City and town life–History–Juvenile literature.
3. Archaeology–Juvenile literature. [1. Cities and
towns–History. 2. City and town life.] I. Title.
HT111.K46 1996
307.76'09–dc20   96-11721
                                                           CIP
                                                           AC

Printed by Wing King Tong, Hong Kong

CONTENTS

INTRODUCTION

Whe people have lived in the same place for a very long time, layers of remains build up as trash collects and buildings get knocked down. Underneath our feet lie layers of history with the oldest at the bottom and the newest at the top. If you could dig down through the soil you would find old objects in the different layers of soil. You can tell the date of each layer by the things found buried in it. This book cuts a slice through a city built on a site where people have lived for thousands of years.

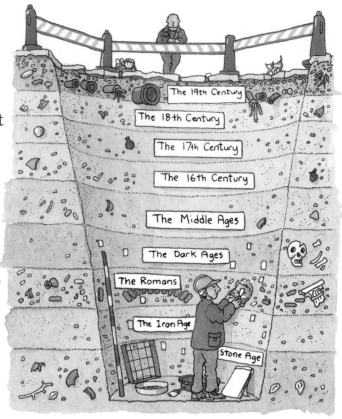

The 19th Century

The 18th Century

The 17th Century

The 16th Century

The Middle Ages

The Dark Ages

The Romans

The Iron Age

Stone Age

FOLLOW THE FAMILY

In a very old city it is quite likely that some families have lived there for hundreds of years, sometimes even in the same house.

In the city in this book there is one family who have lived and worked there throughout the ages. If you look carefully, you can find them on every page. Sometimes their descendants are rich, and sometimes they are quite poor. In every age they have different jobs and wear the fashions of the time. To make them easy to find among the teeming city crowds, they have red hair.

Here they are in costumes from different ages. The man is wearing the sort of clothes worn in the Iron Age, about 200 B.C. The woman is wearing clothes of the Middle Ages, the boy is dressed in a costume of the 17th century, and the girl wears 19th-century fashion.

TREASURE TROVE

Stone axes from the Stone Age were not always rough and crude. Many were polished and ground to a jewel-like finish.

Pots were very useful for storing food and for eating and drinking. Stone Age pots were made from clay and decorated with patterns made with wooden combs. They were then baked hard in a kiln.

In the Iron Age people displayed their wealth as jewelry. A rich person would wear magnificent gold necklaces and armlets called torcs.

The Romans were skilled at making statues. They either cut them in stone or cast them in bronze. Some were huge, designed to stand on monuments or in temples, but many were small ornaments for the home.

The people who dig through the soil to look for remains from our history are called archaeologists. They are very careful when they dig up a site. The place where every object is found, and the objects themselves, are carefully recorded. Photographs are taken and measurements are made.

The things that archaeologists find are very important, as they help us to understand how people lived in the past. When a Stone Age woman threw out a broken pot, she did not realize that her trash would be carefully examined and even glued back together and put on display centuries later.

Even something as small as a button can tell us a lot about the people who made it. It gives us an idea of what sort of clothes they wore, how skilled they were at making things, and, if it is not made of a material found locally, it tells us how far they traveled.

Thousands of objects are buried beneath the city waiting to be dug up, either by accident or by searching archaeologists. If you look carefully through the following city slices, you will find all the things on this page.

It was the fashion in the Middle Ages to have very long and pointed shoes. Some shoes were so long that they had to be tied to the leg with a chain. Shoes then were not made for left and right feet and most had no heels.

Tobacco was first brought to Europe from America in the 16th century. It was smoked in pipes made of baked clay. People thought it was good for their health. They even thought that it kept them from catching the plague!

In the 17th century, cannons fired solid iron balls. The largest weighed nearly 64 pounds (29 kilograms), but 18-pound (8-kilogram) balls were more usual. They are still dug up from old battlefields.

Doctors and pharmacists in the 18th century made their own medicines and sold them in bottles like the one on the right. A blue bottle often meant that the contents were poisonous. Bottled fizzy drinks were popular in the early 19th century. Round-bottomed bottles were stored on their sides to keep the corks moist.

THE STONE AGE

The time over three thousand years ago is called the Stone Age because the tools people used then were made of stone. At the beginning of the Stone Age, people traveled around the countryside with their possessions in search of food. During the last part of the Stone Age, people learned how to grow crops and keep animals, so they could live in one place. They built simple houses of wood, mud, and thatch.

Stone Age people's knives, axes, and scrapers were made out of flint. When they could not find enough flint on the ground, they dug pits to mine it. Needles and small tools were made out of bone. Deer antlers were used as picks, and oxen's shoulder blades as shovels. As stone and bone tools were lost or thrown away they became buried underground. It is the remains of these houses and objects that archaeologists look for today.

COOKING THE STONE AGE WAY

Just imagine how difficult it must be to cook without any metal pots or an oven. This is how it was done in about 2000 B.C.

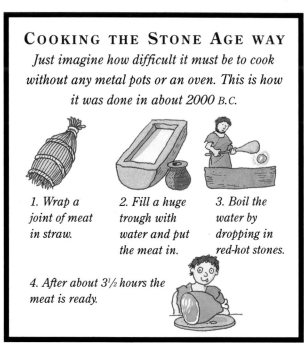

1. Wrap a joint of meat in straw.

2. Fill a huge trough with water and put the meat in.

3. Boil the water by dropping in red-hot stones.

4. After about 3½ hours the meat is ready.

STONE CIRCLES

The greatest monuments of the Stone Age are the stone circles. We do not know the real purpose of these mysterious stones but they were probably used as giant calendars marking the seasons and religious festivals.

At a stone circle in Avebury, England, a skeleton was found under one of the fallen stones. It was the remains of a 17th-century farmer. He was trying to break up the stone when it toppled over and crushed him.

THE IRON AGE

In about 2000 B.C. people discovered how to make tools out of metal. At first they used copper, but this was very soft. Then they learned how to mix tin with copper to make bronze, which was harder. In about 800 B.C., people began to make tools and weapons out of iron, which was the strongest metal of them all.

Iron Age towns were often protected by strong walls made of timber and earth. Houses were larger and more comfortable than they were during the Stone Age. People had learned by now how to weave cloth and make beautiful jewelry out of gold and silver. They sold their goods outside their town, and also bought goods from distant places. Money was used for the first time instead of swapping goods. Iron bars were used as money at first, but later they were replaced by gold coins.

BLUE TATTOOS

The people of the Iron Age painted or tattooed themselves with intricate swirling patterns drawn with a blue vegetable dye called woad.

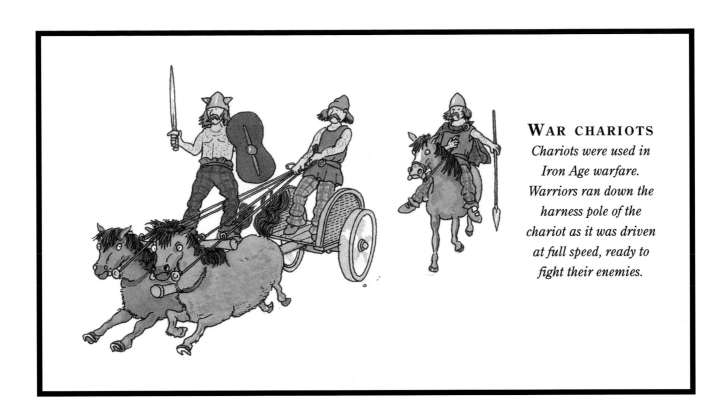

WAR CHARIOTS

Chariots were used in Iron Age warfare. Warriors ran down the harness pole of the chariot as it was driven at full speed, ready to fight their enemies.

THE ROMANS

By about A.D. 100 the mighty Romans had conquered most of Europe and made it part of their vast empire. The Romans put up the first buildings of brick and stone in what is now England and France.

A Roman town had a central market and meeting place called a forum, a town hall, many shops, paved streets, and public baths with hot water and central heating. The bigger towns had several temples, and an amphitheater where games and fights between gladiators took place.

The Romans knew that clean people are healthier and they built sewers and made sure there was a good supply of fresh water for the towns.

SMELLY POTS

Although the Romans were keen on keeping clean, their blocks of apartments must have been very smelly. There were no toilets, and urine was collected in great big pots at the bottom of the stairs. The urine was then sold to clothmakers who used it to stiffen fabric.

WAITING FOR WATER

Only the richest houses had water piped directly into them. Most people got their water from public fountains. These must have been very social places where people gossiped as they waited in line.

HOUSEHOLD GODS

Every Roman home had a shrine and an altar dedicated to the household gods, called the Lares. The head of the family made an offering there every day to keep the gods happy.

KEEPING OUT BURGLARS

The Romans did not have a police force and were worried about being robbed. They built their houses with only a few windows on the walls facing the street, and fitted doors with complicated locks. In many houses, the door was jammed shut with a pole.

THE DARK AGES

In the fifth century A.D., the Roman Empire, which had been growing weaker for a century, was invaded by barbarian tribes from northern Europe. The barbarian tribes that settled within the old Empire—the Goths, Franks, and Saxons—did not want to live in the Roman towns, and the buildings quickly fell into ruin.

The barbarians could not build with stone at first, and their houses were usually made of wood with thatched roofs. The most important building in any village was the hall of the chief, or *thegn*, where he lived with his warriors.

STONE CROSSES

The barbarians were pagans, worshipping many gods, until they were converted to Christianity. One of the first things the Christians did was to erect a stone cross, usually on the site of a pagan holy place. This is where the church was built later.

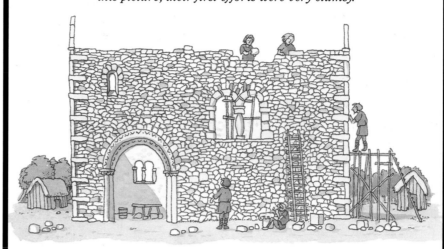

LEARNING TO BUILD

When the Franks and the Saxons began to build with stone in about A.D. 700, they copied the Roman ruins around them. As you can see from this picture, their first efforts were very clumsy.

SAXON TREASURE

The Saxons were skilled jewelry makers. Wealthy men and women wore splendid brooches, clasps, and pendants. These were often made of gold and decorated with glass or colored stones.

THE MIDDLE AGES

During the Middle Ages (roughly 1000 to 1500 A.D.), towns grew and became rich again. Over much of Europe the houses were made of wooden frames with plaster walls. Only castles, churches, and the houses of the very wealthy were built of stone. The streets were often unpaved, with open drains, and it was difficult to keep the town clean. Animals wandered the streets and people threw garbage out of their windows.

The marketplace was very important. People came in from the country to sell food and buy goods made in the town. Shops were simple rooms that opened out onto the street. Almost all of the things people sold in them were made in the house behind the shops.

KEEPING WARM

Most poor people had no fireplaces in their houses. They kept warm with an open fire in a metal grill.

FOOTBALL

A favorite street game was football. Sometimes hundreds played in one game! It was noisy and dangerous— houses were damaged and people were killed.

THE 16TH CENTURY

By the 16th century, houses were larger and had chimneys instead of just a hole in the roof. Most windows were filled with glass for the first time instead of being closed with wooden shutters. Although still built mainly from wood, houses were more comfortable and contained more furniture and ornaments.

The city streets were still unpaved, dirty, and littered with trash. At night the city was dark and often dangerous. Fresh water was taken to houses by a person who worked as a water carrier, or fetched by the family from a fountain (unless the house had a well). There were no drains, though, and during the summer the city was very smelly and unhealthy.

PUBLIC PUNISHMENT

Criminals were often whipped in the streets, or put in the stocks to have rotten vegetables thrown at them.

STREET ENTERTAINMENT

Entertainers such as musicians, jugglers, and people with performing animals earned their living by putting on shows in the streets.

Very few cities survived the 17th century without being wholly or partly destroyed by fire. Often the cause was accidental, but many cities were burned down after being bombarded or captured by enemies. Soldiers who captured cities also badly damaged them as they searched every house for things to steal.

Outbreaks of plague killed thousands of people. The plague was mainly spread by rats who made their nests in the wooden houses and fed on the garbage that lay in the streets.

FIRE FIGHTING

Long hooks pulled burning thatch off roofs. Fire engines were just hand pumps.

MELTING ROOFS

Churches had roofs made out of lead. In a fire, the lead melted and filled the gutters with bright streams of boiling, splashing, molten liquid.

PLAGUE PITS

So many people died from the plague that they were buried together in huge pits.

THE 18TH CENTURY

The great fires of the 17th century meant that many cities were almost completely rebuilt in the 18th century. Most of the old wooden buildings were replaced by houses built of brick and stone. This new style of architecture was based on copies of Roman buildings. Streets were paved and parts of the city began to be less cramped as wide streets and broad squares were built.

SEDAN CHAIRS
Wealthy people took a sedan chair through crowded city streets. These could be hailed like taxis are today.

WATCHMEN

There was still no police force in cities. The streets were patroled by watchmen. A popular sport for young men was knocking over the watchman's shelter and rolling him along the street in it!

FIRE BRIGADES

Iron plates told the private fire brigades that a house was insured with their Fire Assurance Company. If the house wasn't insured with their company, they let it burn down.

5537

THE 19TH CENTURY

During the 19th century, cities changed more than at any other time in their history. They grew much larger and all sorts of different buildings were constructed. There were railway stations, concert halls, libraries, offices, and schools. The streets were paved and brightly lit by gas lamps. Underground pipes carried gas and water into the city and sewage out of the city. Cities became healthier and less smelly places to live, but they suffered from a new problem—traffic jams!

CROSSING SWEEPERS

The streets were covered with horse droppings, mud, and garbage. Poor children earned a little money by sweeping a path across the road for rich people so that they could cross without dirtying their expensive clothes.

STREET LIGHTS

As evening fell, men called lamplighters made their way along the streets with a flame on the end of a long pole, lighting the public gas lamps.

THE 20TH CENTURY

During this century, wars and rebuilding have destroyed many old buildings. Some of those that remain have been altered to suit new uses. Below the streets more tunnels carry extra drains and electricity, telephone, and television cables. Some cities have a public railway

FOUL AIR
In the past, cities were polluted by smells and smoke. Today, cars fill the air with their exhaust fumes.

system deep underground in tunnels. Many buildings now rise to great heights. They have deep foundations to support their weight. Builders digging these foundations sometimes help archaeologists by finding ancient remains in the oldest parts of cities.

29

VIDEO POLICEMEN
Many cities now have video cameras scanning the streets. These help to stop crime.